Pressing Matters

Also by
Caroline Giles Banks

Warm Under the Cat:
Haiku and Senryu Poems

The Clock Chimes:
Haiku and Senryu Poems

The Weight of Whiteness:
A Memoir in Poetry

The Clay Jar:
Haiku, Senryu and Haibun Poems

Tigers, Temples and Marigolds:
Haiku and Haibun Poems

Picture a Poem:
Ekphrastic and Other Poems

PRESSING MATTERS

Haiku, Senryu and Haibun Poems

by **Caroline Giles Banks**

WELLINGTON-GILES PRESS

Minneapolis, Minnesota

United States of America

WELLINGTON-GILES PRESS
10331 Portland Avenue South
Minneapolis, Minnesota 55420
United States of America
wellingtongilespress@gmail.com

Book design by Cate Hubbard
cat7hubb@gmail.com

ISBN 978-0-9645254-9-8
ebook ISBN 979-8-218-14016-8

For
Logan, Tyler and Madi

Contents

Introduction

Pressing Matters: Haiku, Senryu and Haibun, written between 2020 and 2022, responds to the coronavirus pandemic, accelerating changes in the natural environment due to climate change, and worldwide social unrest. Searching for answers to existential questions of loss and survival, the poems concern what it means to be human in a time of profound change and uncertainty.

The haiku, senryu and haibun poems in Part I consider the increasing degradation of the natural environment due to systematic human intervention. Several haibun explore our dependence on nuclear energy and concentrated fossil fuels. Others describe the whipsaw of droughts and deluges. Part II turns to the urgent social issues of economic disparity and insecurity, intolerance and racism, conflict and war. Part III concludes with poems about the COVID-19 pandemic, aging, illness, and death.

Pressing Matters expresses gratitude for the gift of artistic expression and for the power of poetry and the visual arts to nudge our hearts and minds away from despair and complacency towards engagement and hope.

I

call it what you will
late fall
roses still in bloom

sweet tea
honeybee and me
in clover

her dance card full
of admirers
showy lady slipper

Queen Anne's lace
deep curtsies
to the rain

iris lily rose van Gogh models still life

fossil flower once ephemeral leaves a trace behind

elopement bouquet
Black-eyed Susans
wild like her

pine bamboo plum
three friends of winter
greet sled mittens cocoa

> *Three Friends of Winter* by
> Yamamoto Baiitsu
> Japanese, 19th century
> ink on paper, Minneapolis Institute of Art

sweet scent of lilacs
lost to COVID
found in its color blue

deadheading the petal not ready to let go let go

Round and Roundabout

Wanting to avoid crowded airports, planes, and COVID-19, I take my first road trip in many years. Oklahoma in August. Seeking respite from the 100+ degrees heat, the AC is on full blast. I've set the cruise control to 78 MPH, just above the limit of 75, but not high enough to avoid the whiplash of passing trucks. I am amazed to see acres and acres of wind farms, gigantic blades pinwheeling "new" energy far over the horizon. Beneath these megaliths a few fantastical rust-brown birds mechanically peck the earth, hungry for liquid gold buried ever deeper in the ground.

> car trip
> tank filled on credit
> fossil remains

Tribal casinos hug the interstate, oases offering a buffet, a suite, luck for those who stop, and jobs, revenue for resource-deprived Choctaw, Chickasaw, and Cherokee. Needing a break, I take the off-ramp to the Broken Bow casino. Masked up I wait in line for sweet tea and wonder if another road trip is in the cards.

> rock paper scissors
> trying to keep a hand
> in the game

Muddy Waters

The Hiawatha Golf Course, built in the 1930s, sits on drained wetlands near the confluence of the Mississippi and Minnesota Rivers. To prevent frequent flooding and erosion of the course, the Minneapolis Park and Recreation Board proposes to redesign and reduce it to half its current size. Claiming the floodplain as ancestral land subject to early 19th-century treaty rights, the Anishinaabe Dakota wish to return the area to wetlands for wild rice fields, clean water, and natural habitat.

> First Nations'
> prehistoric pictographs
> high-water marks

The golf course is also one of the first racially integrated courses in the city's park system. Many Black golfers consider it their "home" golf course and want to keep all of its 18 holes open for future recreation. The human family is diverse, multi-cultural, and, for some, recognizes all living things as "kin." A seemingly mundane land use problem, the future of the golf course raises important issues of equity, fairness, and inclusivity, requiring education, dialogue, and a willingness to find compromise.

> traps and hazards
> staying the course
> the fair way

covering titles
in the window display
bookstore cats

cat gone
switching off
easy-listening radio

still topping
the T. Rex hit list
birdsong

wild turkeys strut the city
gobble food...
giving thanks

fledglings cozy down in cottonwood cotton

the boulevard tree's
understory
sidewalk chalk

maple leaves fall impressed in cement

gone before the pail is full strawberry moon

flight cancellations
overheated birds
fall from the sky

Water Wars

Water is scarce in the foothills of the Sangre de Cristo
Mountains in northern New Mexico. Gardens that
depend on snowmelt to grow red and green chili peppers
are withering.

Descendants of early Spanish settlers in the area rely on
centuries-old traditions to decide where and when sluice
gates along the narrow earthen irrigation canals are raised
or lowered to distribute water among villagers. Drought,
as well as economic and demographic changes, threaten
these local customs for allocating water. Water Boards,
often lobbied by outside developers, now weigh the utility,
equity, and fairness of traditional customs.

> snowpack almost depleted
> don't dam it
> damn it

Conservation of scarce resources—or growth and
development? Wooden buckets and sluice gates—
or PVC pipes and metal faucets? Stay local—or go global?
In the meantime

> the Rio Grande
> trickles down
> to a misnomer

Temperatures Rising

Images of uprooted trees and drowned houses scroll
nonstop across my screen. 1,000-year rain "events" in
Dallas, Las Vegas, St. Louis, Phoenix, Jackson, West Virginia,
Eastern Kentucky, California, and more sweep people and
pets into culverts, onto rooftops, and under bridges. No time
to bag grains of sand, to grab a To Go Bag. It makes me weep.

> sick Earth
> triage and treatment
> in the waiting room

Droughts and deluges disturb habitats of other species,
too, changing our interface with them. Breaking news from
the W.H.O.: malaria, dengue, cholera, plague, Zika, anthrax,
typhoid, and other infectious diseases are on the rise
worldwide, worsened by climate hazards.

> rubble and debris
> neonatal incubators
> for no-see-ums

backyard rain gauge
half-empty half-full
open mind

dry spell
no ripples
in the frog pond

plastic bottles and bags
float out to sea
passing the buck

The Eye of the Beholder
In the Company of Burtynsky and Bashō

Edward Burtynsky's photographs are stories of human
alterations to the Earth. Taken using drones and fixed-wing
aircraft these depict large-scale industrial projects and their
effect on the environment. I am especially drawn to a photo
of the tailings pond of an African diamond mine. Seen from
the air, it appears almost beautiful, like a massive flower
with its black-and-white petals opened and impressed upon
the ground. I am reminded of Bashō's words:

> *How admirable!*
> *to see lightning and not think*
> *life is fleeting*
>
> Translation by Robert Hass
> *The Essential Haiku: Verses*
> *of Bashō, Buson and Issa.*
> New Jersey: The Ecco Press, 1994

Harvest Moon
raking algae blooms
under the dock

citywide blackout
night sky wonders
to wonder

the nearness of you stardust

radiation exposure
To Go Bag
CBD gummies

Ground Zero

As a child in Japan Arata Isozaki (1931–2022) saw the
utter destruction of Hiroshima. In a flash the city, devoid
of buildings, became an emptiness asking for possibilities.
How does an architect who knows the transience of cities
and the eventuality of their decay design for the future?
I consider Isozaki's sublime Art Tower Mito, completed in
1990. This iconic 100-meter-tall structure is comprised of
many triangular pyramids stacked in varying orientations.
Like a jazz riff of seeming contradictions the titanium tower
appears to twist and turn, a shiny silver megalith reflecting
that and this, after and before.

dreams

sift

into

fissures

between

memories

Hiding in Plain Sight

The meltdown of Chernobyl's nuclear power plant in 1986
is attributed to "design flaws" and "human error."
Euphemisms such as these can't begin to disguise or
mitigate the existential threat to our planet by radioactive
contaminants. To "contain" the radiation the damaged
reactor was entombed in a concrete and steel "sarcophagus."
This language draws my mind away from death and disease
and transports it 4,500 years back in time to pharaohs,
pyramids, and mummies, the stuff of museums, film, and
fantasy. In 2016 the reactor was re-entombed and the
"alienation" zone around it was increased to 1,000 square
miles. The timetable for its future "habitability" is now
estimated to be between hundreds and tens of thousands
of years. "What"–there likely is no recognizable "who"–
will take these future readings of radioactivity?

> blind man's buff
> underplaying
> we all are "it"

The Man of the Hole

His hut hidden in the rainforest from outsiders, the last
known member of an Amazonian tribe is found lying in
his hammock covered in feathers. Decades earlier those
greedy for the tribe's land and resources murdered
almost all his kin with poisoned sugar. Like a keepsake
wedding suit, the funereal garb of brilliant bird feathers
reflects planning and preparation, readiness and ritual.
His death is a harbinger of the accelerating annihilation
and disappearance of untold numbers of cultures and
peoples— not unlike the mass extinction of other species—
due to the cumulative effects of deliberative and systematic
human activity.

> gone
> one by one bye one
> time flies

II

dealt the white card
wanting to play
just hearts

Say Their Names

Boston tea party
leaves oversteeped
in salt water

pipeline nixed First Peoples dance to the sun

protest sign
wanting to overcome
semantics

nurses burnout
triage and treatment
on the picket line

news of freedom late edition Juneteenth

selfie
wearing a gas mask
vanitas

Loss and Damage

telegraph pole
to boulevard trees
ghost stories

furniture and undertaking business diversification

deadheading blossoms
still no news
about the bank loan

Quinceañera gold
pawning off her girlhood
to help pay bills

farmer makes ends meet taxidermy and cheese

pressing issue
garment workers strike
while the irons are hot

Wall Street
Photograph by Paul Strand, 1915

A chiaroscuro warning shot in stark black and white.
Dwarfed by the massive bank building– its windows
recessed, nonreflective, impenetrable– faceless city
workers stride along the sidewalk into the shadowland
of the Great War and Depression. A century later, with
its toxic mix of a senseless war, ongoing pandemic, and
rapid inflation, I ask, "Are we in recession?"

> umbrella unfurled
> before the storm–
> fool me once

On Pointe

A toe shoe. The jagged hem of a tutu. A once graceful hand.
Bits and pieces of the bronze statue of Marjorie Tallchief,
Osage Nation prima ballerina (1926–2021), are recovered
in a Tulsa, Oklahoma scrapyard. The vandalism of the
statue, one of five sculptures of Native American ballerinas
featured in the Tulsa Historical Society and Museum's
installation known as the "Five Moons," not only outrages
aficionados of classical ballet but also reopens memories
of the fiery destruction of Tulsa's "Black Wall Street"
100 years ago. The sculptor pledges to repair and recreate
the statue with the found fragments and original mold
and to return Marjorie to the installation.

> beauty reborn
> in kindled forge
> Firebird

girl with a shiner
on her chain
the peace sign

also lying prone
on the sidewalk
peonies

white lilies
wither on sidewalks
another mass shooting

open house
the realtor nixes
the BLM sign

Grim Reaper scything green new deals

Vrbo
turning the President's photo
to the wall

staging the farm for sale tasseled corn

nut truck heist
the pecan case
hard to crack

duck and cover drills
early education
in big lies

screeching rails
Dad leaves
for boot camp

SCOTUS
weight watchers
recalibrate the scales

round and roundabout the ballot drop box

Jan. 6
halyards slap the flagpole
epiphany

Words Beyond Wars

War tramples Kyiv culture.
The art museum's windows are blown out.
The concert hall is shrouded in dust.
The statue of Taras Shevchenko, lauded poet,
is pitted and pocked by bullets. Dead silence.
These images beg my imagination
for color, for sound, this pen.

        ringing the base
        of the bell tower
        sprouts of green grass

Call and Response

The barrage of images from Ukraine is heartbreaking. My pen is shell-shocked into paralysis. Blank sheets of paper on my desk are white flags of surrender to complacency, silence, and remorse. Then I see **CHILDREN** plainly written with the white paint of innocence on the grounds of the drama theater in Mariupol where women and youth have taken shelter. As a mother and grandmother I am summoned by this single word, this cry, this plea, this entreaty to spare the innocent and to safeguard the future. An image, a word lifts the fog of war. We all are children. Children: thusness of hope.

> rockets can't read
> their names
> 109 empty strollers

Flight and Fight

9/11 migration
wondering what else
the geese know

Resolute Desk eagle eyes arrows of war

bald eagle stays frosty
between forays
broken olive branch

night vision
last one out
shrouded in green light

clear skin bandages all wounds matter

Peace Garden
on the weeping willow
1,000 cranes

Statues Also Breathe
Sculptures by Prune Nourry, 2022

As they prepared for science exams in 2014 several
hundred Chibok girls were abducted by Boko Haram
from the Government Girls Secondary School in Nigeria.
Reminiscent of slavery in the United States, the captive girls
are prohibited from possessing or reading books. Inspired
by ancient Nigerian Ife terra-cotta heads, the French artist
Prune Nourry, in collaboration with 108 students from
Obafemi-Awolowo University and family members of the
abducted girls, produced 108 clay-head sculptures of the
missing girls. Defying Boko Haram's strictures to isolate
women and girls, Nourry exhibits the sculptures as an
indivisible group, outdoors, in public: bold rows of girls,
a readied "army," a defiant "platoon" of girls. As I look at
their noble faces, resolute facial expressions, and distinct
hair patterns I am mindful of the worldwide threat to girls'
education and self-determination. I join them as an ally
and uncap my pen.

> books in plain jackets
> safe and secure
> under burkas

Clarion Call

Hagia Sophia, the magnificent complex in Istanbul, was built
in the 6th century as a Christian church, then repurposed
as a mosque in the 15th century during the Ottoman Empire.
Under Ataturk, founder of the secular Republic of Turkey,
it opened in 1935 as a museum, before becoming a mosque
again in 2020.

> prayer rugs
> beside Doric columns
> bending the same knee

Ever reminding us of Christianity's and Islam's shared
historical origins, the syncretic amalgamation of mosaics
depicting Christianity with soaring minarets is an enduring
testament to the power of art and architecture to reflect our
common humanity in the face of cultural diversity, conflict,
and change.

> Xmas cacti bud
> in Ramadan
> shared roots

thunder bolt
digital clocks flash
12 12 12

the green comet
last visible
to Neanderthals too

III

newfound DNA cousins Neanderthals

Ma's cookbook
enough splatters
for soup

teapot shards
glued together
Dad's shaky hand

embers smolder
still using my ex's
last name

altering the seam
between that and this
Ma's scissors

she knows all about me
the fortune teller's dress
just like Ma's

Ties That Bind

Ma, wheelchair-bound for many years,
looks forward to her daily swim. Today
I'm her mooring anchor buoy in the pool.
Our time is cut short by a fast moving cold front
and rain storm. Fearing lightning strikes and hypothermia,
I grasp Ma under her arms, lift her up and over the coping,
and place her in the wheelchair. Wavering on the door sill
she is washed and wrapped in folds of cascading water.

       newborn
       on the threshold
       eternity's embrace

pop-up ad
I might also like
my new book

selfies before and after
the face lift
Vanitas

rough drafts
pronouns orbit
the recycling bin

bio-redux slash/pronouns

twists and turns
new lead loaded
in the pencil

books in plain jackets
safe and sound
in the tree house

thirst quenched
sipping from Chiyo-ni's
well bucket

horizon line
Calliope's causeway
from there to here

musesee'em

shirt buttons
     a
      s
     k
      e
    w
fall back time

All Souls' Day
ants savor tamales
beside the tombstone

New Year's party
my lover's wife
brings flowers

White Coat Ceremony
selfies placed
in bio-hazard bags

Inside the Lines

Legal pads, yellow ones with thin pale blue rumble strips
to keep a pen in line, remain my choice for writing early
drafts. I still keep a landline to hear a longed-for human
voice and, perhaps, the giggle of a baby or a cat's meow.
When asked at the start of a virtual workshop how I wish
to be addressed I enter *Ms./Dr.* in the chat. I notice that
others have posted s*he/her, he/him, they/them* and am
reminded that marital status and academic credentials
are no longer the preferred criteria for self-identity
among younger generations.

> earthbound
> not yet
> in the cloud

plant-based wings
they who grill
cry foul

boosted into orbit
sweet payload
of Mars bars

fasting
there is no fat
in heaven

following orders
to stay-at-home
kneading dough

virtual Thanksgiving
finally
at the grown-ups' table

matching Zoom blouse
and face mask
the cat's meow

family meeting
waiting to tell mom
you're muted

Zoom chat
the sound
of one hand clapping

cruise of a lifetime in cabin lockdown

vaccines
the gravedigger
makes a U-turn

hanging on
the rearview mirror
face mask

Smartwatches blood oxygen falls SOS

engraver's family discount
the date after the dash
blank

widow keeping her hair long for him

widower
the unevenness
of his sideburns

address book
each year erasing
friends and family

Shelf Life

Tired from picking blackberries
I rest under the mature maple tree.
Lowering my titanium knees onto the grass
I see gray-brown shelves of hardened discs
wrapped around the base of its trunk.
Like your rings, do the shelves count the years?
Can tea and tinctures from your compounds
heal my wounds? Next summer will I still see
my name etched onto your brackets?

        whistling a blade of grass
        under the Mother Tree
        thusness of hope

treble cleft notes
hitched in syncopation
Moonshadow   moon shadow

playing cards
clipped to bike spokes
song cycles

picture poems muse see'em

Polyglot

I don't remember touching any of the buttons on the
3 remotes required for operating the Smart TV. But "it"
decided that I have suddenly become visually impaired
and require play-by-play description of the action on the
screen. In a monotone A.I. dialect "it" says: *He enters the
room. He takes off his hat. She steps forward and shakes
his hand.* Then the dialogue code-switches from English
to a Romance language. Drawing on years of studying Latin
I attempt to translate but quickly tire of the exercise.

What I really want is help installing the pricey new sound bar.

> the languages
> of getting old
> FaceTime with grandkids

hangover sun salutation to the streetlamp

polka dots caught
in infinity's net
hallucinations

      untitled by Kusama Yayoi, 1967
      oil on canvas, Minneapolis Institute of Art

already familiar
with social distancing
the royal cortege

50th reunion
the photographer asks us
to lift our chins

wedding march steps
getting to know
my new knee

cataracts removed color and clarity returned

angiogram
my broken heart
undetected

hands over heart
under the sheet
dress rehearsal

the clay jar
some day
holding me

Acknowledgments

The author acknowledges the editors of the following anthologies, journals, and magazines for publication of the poems listed below, some in slightly modified form. Copyright © by Caroline Giles Banks.

Caroline Giles Banks, "call it what you will," *bottle rockets* #38 (2016).

—,"sweet tea," *Haiku Dialogue* (08/03/2022).

—, "her dance card full," *Haiku Dialogue* (05/11/2022).

—, "Queen Anne's lace," *Haiku Dialogue* (08/10/2022).

—, "elopement bouquet," *Haiku Dialogue* (2022).

—, "pine bamboo plum," *Haiku Dialogue* (10/20/2021).

—, "sweet scent of lilacs," *Haiku Dialogue* (05/18/2022).

—, "deadheading the petal," *Haiku Dialogue* (08/24/2022).

—, "Round and Roundabout," *Contemporary Haibun Online* 17:3 (Dec 2021).

—, "Muddy Waters," *Drifting Sands Haibun* #17 (September 2022).

—, "covering titles," *Haiku Dialogue* (03/09/2022).

—, "cat gone," *Window Seats, A Contemporary Anthology of Cat Haiku and Senryu*, ed. Stanford M. Forrester, 2021.

—, "still topping," *tsuri-doro* #5 (Sept/Oct 2021).

—, "wild turkeys strut the city," *The Daily Double Haiku* (11/16/2022).

—, "the boulevard tree's," *Haiku Dialogue* (05/04/2022).

—, "gone before the pail," *Modern Haiku* 52:3 (Autumn 2021).

—, "the Rio Grande," *tsuri-doro* #13 (Jan/Feb 2023).

—, "dry spell," *Haiku Dialogue* (01/25/2023).

—, "The Eye of the Beholder," *Drifting Sands Haibun* #19 (January 2023).

—, "the nearness of you," *Haiku Dialogue* (11/10/2021).

—, "radiation exposure," *tsuri-doro* #12 (Nov/Dec 2022).

—, "Hiding in Plain Sight," *Drifting Sands Haibun* #18 (November 2022).

—, "The Man of the Hole," *The Babylon Sidedoor* (October 2022).

—, "dealt the white card," *tsuri-doro* #6 (Nov/Dec 2021).

—, "Boston tea party," *Haiku Dialogue* (10/13/2021).

—, "protest sign," *bottle rockets* #44 (2021).

—, "nurses burnout," *bottle rockets* #48 (2023).

—, "furniture and undertaking," *failed haiku,Volume*6 Issue #70 (2021).

—, "deadheading blossoms," *Earth Signs, Haiku North America Anthology*, 2017.

—, "quinceañera gold," *bottle rockets* #45 (2021).

—, "farmer makes ends meet," *failed haiku,Volume*6 Issue #70 (2021).

—, "pressing issue," *failed haiku,Volume*6 Issue #70 (2021).

—, *"Wall Street,"* The Babylon Sidedoor (December 2022).

—, "girl with a shiner," *tsuri-doro* #11 (Sept/Oct 2022).

—, "also lying prone," *tsuri-doro* #1 (Jan/Feb 2021).

—, "white lilies," *Haiku Dialogue* (06/22/2022) and *failed haiku,Volume*7 Issue #82 (Oct 2022).

—, "open house," *on down the road, HSA 2017 Members' Anthology*, 2017.

—, "Vrbo," *A Moment's Longing, HSA Members' Anthology*, 2019.

—, "staging the farm," *tsuri-doro* #9 (May/June 2022).

—, "duck and cover drills," *Haiku Dialogue* (07/13/2022).

—, "screeching rails," *Haiku Dialogue* (12/14/2022).

—, "SCOTUS," *tsuri-doro* #8 (March/April 2022).

—, "Jan. 6," *tsuri-doro* #7 (Jan/Feb 2022).

—, "Call and Response," *Drifting Sands Haibun* #15 (May 2022) and *failed haiku,Volume*7 Issue #83 (Nov 2022).

—, "9/11 migration," *frogpond* 25:3 (2002).

—, "clear skin bandages," *The Haiku Way To Healing: Illness, Injury and Pain*, ed. Robert Epstein, 2022.

—, "Peace Garden," *Haiku Dialogue* (10/27/2021).

—, "Statues Also Breathe," *Drifting Sands Haibun* #20 (March 2023).

—, "Clarion Call," *The Babylon Sidedoor* (December 2022).

—, "prayer rugs," *tsuri-doro* #10 (July/August 2022).

___, "thunder bolt," *failed haiku,Volume*8 Issue #86 (Feb 2023).

—, "newfound DNA cousins," *Visiting the Wind, HSA Members' Anthology*, 2021.

—, "Ma's cookbook," *failed haiku,Volume*7 Issue #81 (Sept 2022).

—, "teapot shards," *Haiku Dialogue* (09/15/2021).

—, "embers smolder," *failed haiku,Volume*6 Issue #71 (2021).

—, "she knows all about me," *Haiku Dialogue* (12/28/2022).

—, "selfies before and after," *Haiku Dialogue* (09/29/2021).

—, "rough drafts," *Haiku Dialogue* (11/24/2021) and *failed haiku,Volume*8 Issue #87 (March 2023).

—, "twists and turns," *Haiku Dialogue* (01/11/2023).

—, "books in plain jackets," *Haiku Dialogue* (01/04/2023).

—, "thirst quenched," *Haiku Dialogue* (11/03/2021).

—, "musesee'em," *Whiptail Journal* Issue #5 (Nov 2022).

—, "shirt buttons," *failed haiku,Volume*6 Issue #71 (2021).

—, "All Souls' Day," *Haiku Dialogue* (11/02/2022).

—, "New Year's party," *failed haiku,Volume*5 Issue #60 (Dec 2020) and *THF Per Diem/Haiku of the Day* (January 3, 2023).

—, "Inside the Lines," *Contemporary Haibun Online* 18:1 (April 2022).

—, "plant-based wings," *failed haiku,Volume*8 Issue #87 (March 2023).

—, "fasting," *Haiku Dialogue* (12/15/ 2021).

—, "following orders," *frogpond* 43:3 (fall 2020) and *dawn returns, HSA Members' Anthology*, 2022.

—, "virtual Thanksgiving," *frogpond* 44:1 (winter 2021).

—, "matching Zoom blouse," *Haiku Dialogue* (07/27/2022).

—, "family meeting," *Haiku Dialogue* (11/16/2022).

—, "Zoom chat," *2021 Haiku North America Anthology*, 2021.

—, "cruise of a lifetime," *Haiku Dialogue* (10/26/2022).

—, "vaccines," *The Haiku Way to Healing: Illness, Injury and Pain*, ed. Robert Epstein, 2022.

—, "hanging on," *Modern Haiku* 51:3 (Autumn 2020) and *failed haiku,Volume*8 Issue #85 (2023).

—, "engraver's family discount," *Haiku Dialogue* (06/29/2022).

—, "widower," *frogpond* 38:2 (spring/summer 2015) and *failed haiku,Volume*6 Issue #67 (July 2021).

—, "address book," *bottle rockets* #33 (2015).

—, "treble cleft notes," *Haiku Dialogue* (09/22/2021).

—, "playing cards," *Haiku Dialogue* (12/21/2022).

—, "picture poems," *tsuri-doro* #11 (Sept/Oct 2022).

—, "Polyglot," *The Babylon Sidedoor* (January 2022).

—, "polka dots caught," *Haiku Dialogue* (01/26/2022).

—, "already familiar," *tsuri-doro* #4 (July/Aug 2021).

—, "50th reunion," *bottle rockets* #35 (2016).

—, "wedding march steps," *Pulse, Voices From the Heart of Medicine* (May 2021).

—, "angiogram," *The Clay Jar: Haiku, Senryu and Haibun Poems*, Caroline Giles Banks, 2013 and *The Haiku Way To Healing: Illness, Injury and Pain*, ed. Robert Epstein, 2022.

—, "hands over heart," *Haiku Dialogue* (12/22/2021).

—, "the clay jar," *The Clay Jar: Haiku, Senryu and Haibun Poems*, Caroline Giles Banks, 2013.

About the Author

Caroline Giles Banks, born in Boston, Massachusetts, was educated at Wellesley College, the University of New Mexico, the University of Minnesota, and the University of Chicago. Dr. Banks is a cultural anthropologist by training and profession and was on the faculties of the University of Wisconsin-River Falls and Luther College in Decorah, Iowa. Her poetry is often informed by her anthropological training and research. She is the author of *Warm Under the Cat: Haiku and Senryu Poems*; *The Clock Chimes: Haiku and Senryu Poems*; *The Weight of Whiteness: A Memoir in Poetry*; *The Clay Jar: Haiku, Senryu and Haibun Poems*; *Tigers, Temples and Marigolds: Haiku and Haibun Poems*; and *Picture a Poem: Ekphrastic and Other Poems*. Her award-winning poems have been published in numerous anthologies, literary magazines and journals. She lives in Minneapolis, Minnesota.